# Hello, Travelers!

Are you ready for your next trip? Hunt through this pad of adventures and see if you can pack up the answers in these three activities. Ready, set, go!

## You'll need snacks for the road.

How many of each can you find?

banana

carrot

pizza

## Which of these types of transportation can you find the most of?

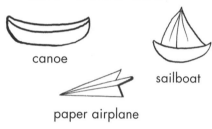

canoe

paper airplane

sailboat

## You'll need plenty of clean clothes for the journey.

Can you find these hidden clothing items?

mitten

glove

sock

propeller hat

Cover art by Pat Lewis

# Hidden Pictures®

Write a number below each object based on the order in which you find it in the big picture. Then flip the page to create a silly story with the objects!

mushroom
◯

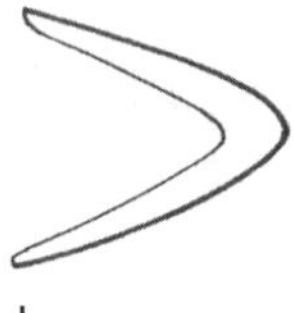

boomerang
◯

toothbrush
◯

butter knife
◯

crescent moon
◯

wishbone
◯

lemon
◯

button
◯

paper airplane
◯

elf's hat
◯

taco shell
◯

magnet
◯

## BONUS
Can you also find these objects?

ring

needle

pear

pickle

# Road Trip

Art by Gary Mohrman

Flip the page!

# Road Trip

*Write the object names in the numbered spaces. For example, if you found the mushroom first, write "mushroom" in the first blank.*

When Mom and Dad said we'd be driving in an old

_____ across Route _____,
        1                                        2

I thought it would be *ruff*, but so far it's been a treat!

My sister and I rolled down the _____
                                              3

and boy did the air smell different. Being in the middle

of the _____ feels like we are riding in
                 4

the back of a rickety _____ exploring
                                    5

the Wild Wild _____. When we passed
                            6

a giant _____, Dad shouted
                        7

"_____!" Mom wanted to stop and take a
       8

picture, so we turned the _____ around.

9

We hopped out and posed for a family picture.

Just as the camera snapped a photo, a great big

_____ blew right past us! The timing was

10

perfect. Now it's back to the open _____.

11

Next stop, the _____ Museum!

12

# Hidden Pictures®

Write a number below each object based on the order in which you find it in the big picture. Then flip the page to create a silly story with the objects!

sock ◯

spoon ◯

scissors ◯

doughnut ◯

pizza ◯

envelope ◯

crown ◯

lollipop ◯

pear ◯

carrot ◯

canoe ◯

book ◯

**BONUS**
Can you also find these objects?

ice-cream cone

needle

# Setting Sail

Art by Paula Becker

Flip the page!

# Setting Sail

*Write the object names in the numbered spaces. For example, if you found the doughnut first, write "doughnut" in the first blank.*

Ahoy, matey! I'm showing these young buccaneers

the ropes—or how to tie them, rather. After two

days of _____-mapping lessons and
<br>1

_____-digging practice, they're ready to
<br>2

hunt for Blackbeard's long lost _____.
<br>3

This may be the fiercest group of pirates to ever sail

the _____ seas. Tomorrow we'll climb
<br>4

aboard the Blue _____. She's a beaut'
<br>5

with her crisp _____ sails and sturdy
<br>6

_____. Once we set sail, we'll locate the
<br>7

Isle of _____ right off the shimmery coast

8

of _____. Luckily my _____

9                                        10

compass never fails to point me in the right direction.

An old pirate's superstition is to tap it three times and

say "_____" before lifting anchor. Shiver

11

me timbers! Look at the _____. Time to

12

heave ho!

# Hidden Pictures®

Write a number below each object based on the order in which you find it in the big picture. Then flip the page to create a silly story with the objects!

mushroom ◯

canoe ◯

ax ◯

doughnut ◯

envelope ◯

book ◯

fishhook ◯

hockey stick ◯

worm ◯

football ◯

bowling pin ◯

straw ◯

**BONUS**
Can you also find these objects?

tack

die

# Space Explorers

Art by Catherine Copeland

Flip the page!

# Space Explorers

*Write the object names in the numbered spaces. For example, if you found the worm first, write "worm" in the first blank.*

## Captain's Log: Day 18 on the

_____ **Voyager**
1

In fifteen days, we'll reach Planet _____
2

and see the cosmic _____. It'll be out of
3

this world! Astronaut Bearld and I just navigated the

ship to safety through the _____ asteroids
4

that were nearly the size of _____
5

boulders on Mt. _____. We got so close
6

to the _____ that we had to put on our
7

_____ sunglasses. At last, we can now
8

relax, turn off the _____ switch, and put
9

up our paws, except for Hoppy and Toto who are

fixing the _____ that came loose. Later
10

we'll all play a game of pin the _____
11

on the _____ vent. This is Commander
12

Catticus signing off.

# Hïdden Pïctures®

Write a number below each object based on the order in which you find it in the big picture. Then flip the page to create a silly story with the objects!

mitten

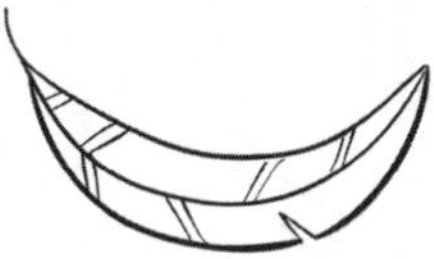

feather

pushpin

pencil

bread

magnifying glass

ice-cream cone

snowman

key

toothbrush

wastebasket

carrot

## BONUS
Can you also find these objects?

paintbrush

fork

rabbit

banana

worm

# Happy Trails

Art by Jennifer Harney

Flip the page!

# Happy Trails

*Write the object names in the numbered spaces. For example, if you found the pencil first, write "pencil" in the first blank.*

It's hiking day! My brother Garret and I are hiking

the _____ trails with Aunt Rose and
<u>1</u>

Uncle Tim. They both know these trails like the back

of their _____ because they're nearly
<u>2</u>

right in their backyard. Every morning they grab

their hiking _____ and walk with their
<u>3</u>

golden retriever Mr. _____ through the
<u>4</u>

_____ Forest. So far today we've found
<u>5</u>

deer, possum, and _____ tracks. A snake
<u>6</u>

or tarantula wouldn't scare me, but I never want to see

a giant _____ stare me in the face! When

7

we reached _____ Falls, Garret got a

8

little too close to the _____. A big gust

9

of wind blew off his _____ hat, and the

10

dog jumped right into the water to retrieve it. When

he brought it back to Garret, Uncle Tim said, "That's

a good _____!" and patted him on the

11

_____. I just love the great outdoors!

12

# Hidden Pictures®

Write a number below each object based on the order in which you find it in the big picture. Then flip the page to create a silly story with the objects!

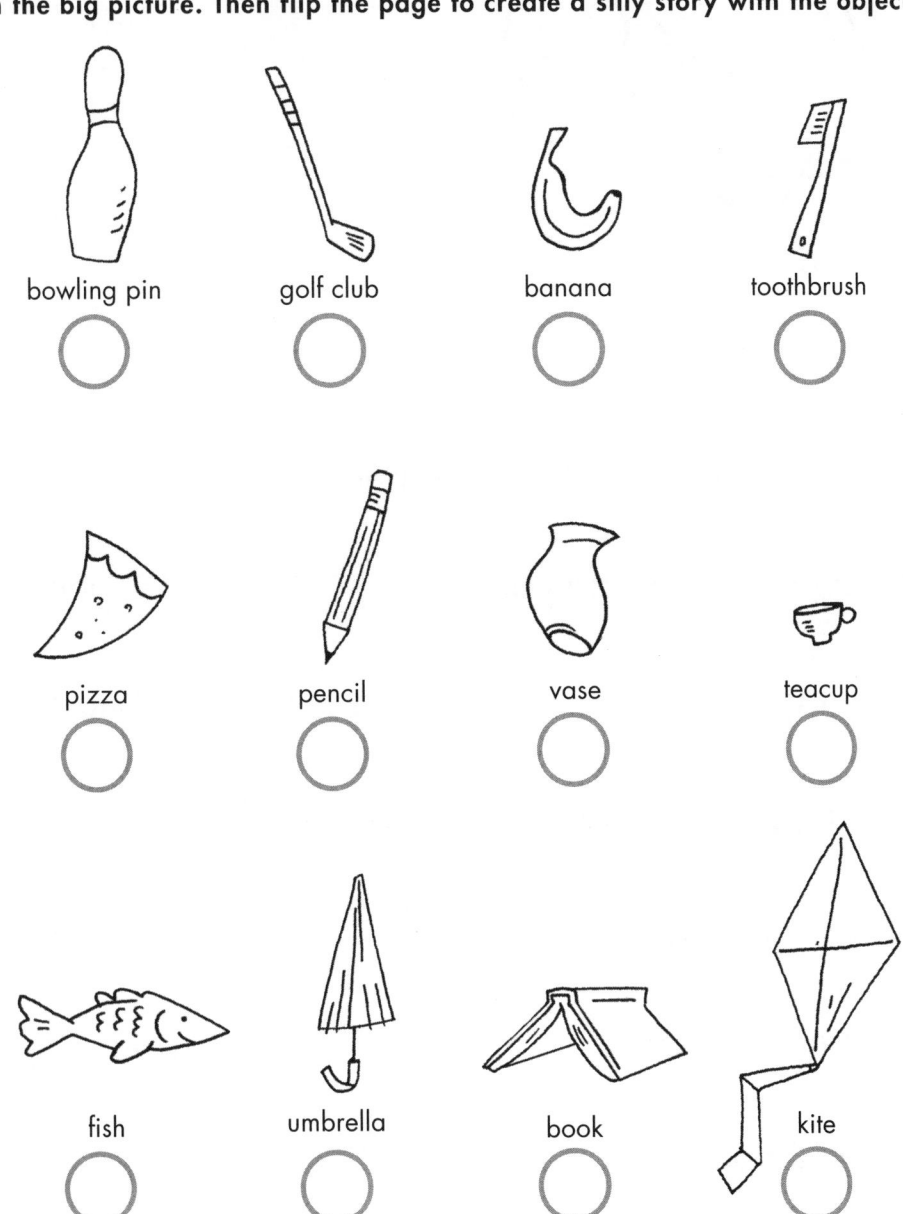

bowling pin

golf club

banana

toothbrush

pizza

pencil

vase

teacup

fish

umbrella

book

kite

# To Grandma's House

Flip the page!

# To Grandma's House

*Write the object names in the numbered spaces. For example, if you found the golf club first, write "golf club" in the first blank.*

Every winter we take a sleigh ride in the jingly

_____ all the way to Grandma's

     1

_____. Grandma greets us with a big

     2

hug and warm mug of hot _____,

                        3

and then she shouts, "It's _____ time!"

                 4

Mom grabs the _____-shaped cookie

          5

cutters while Dad grabs the _____ tray.

              6

We fill the preheated _____ with as

          7

many trays as will fit. When the _____

              8

dings, my brother, sister, and I decorate every single

_____. Sometimes I accidentally frost my

9

_____ more than the cookies. Oops! As

10

a special surprise, I brought my grandma's favorite

_____ sprinkles for the sugar cookies.

11

They'll sure make them stand out. I'll make sure to save

a delicious _____ for the pony to snack

12

on for the way home—that is if my sister doesn't eat

them all it first!

# Hidden Pictures®

Write a number below each object based on the order in which you find it in the big picture. Then flip the page to create a silly story with the objects!

anchor ◯

toaster ◯

canoe ◯

banana ◯

book ◯

hammer ◯

magnet ◯

mushroom ◯

harmonica ◯

ladder ◯

sock ◯

toothbrush ◯

# Great Bear Lodge

SPECIAL HIBERNATION RATES

Art by Neil Numberman

Flip the page!

# Great Bear Lodge

*Write the object names in the numbered spaces. For example, if you found the anchor first, write "anchor" in the first blank.*

Come and visit the Great Bear Lodge where you

can kick back and sleep the winter away in our

sensational _____ hotel. Our gold-
　　　　　　　　　　1

_____ amenities and spacious suites
　　　2

overlooking the _____ provide you with
　　　　　　　　　　3

everything hibernation has to offer. Stretch out those

claws in our luxurious, grizzly-sized _____
　　　　　　　　　　　　　　　　　　4

beds. Or if you're looking for superior comfort, the

polar-_____ bed is just for you. We offer
　　　　5

a complimentary _____ when you arrive,
　　　　　　　　　6

along with an all-you-can-eat _____

7

buffet. We guarantee you won't have a growling

_____ interrupting your slumber. And upon

8

request, we provide top-notch earplugs if your loved one

happens to snore like a blaring _____.

9

We pride ourselves in giving the highest level of

service to our _____ guests. When

10

you leave, you'll be as refreshed as a sun-kissed

_____ on a springtime _____.

11                                              12

Book your reservation today!

# Hidden Pictures®

Write a number below each object based on the order in which you find it in the big picture. Then flip the page to create a silly story with the objects!

paintbrush ◯

mushroom ◯

banana ◯

dog bone ◯

ruler ◯

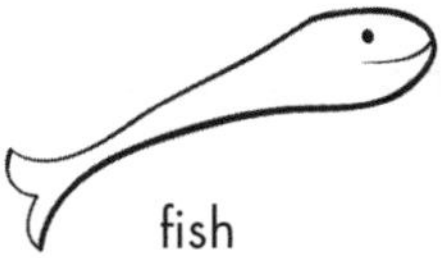

fish ◯

paper clip ◯

bell ◯

doughnut ◯

chili pepper ◯

hairpin ◯

kite ◯

**BONUS**
Can you also find these objects?

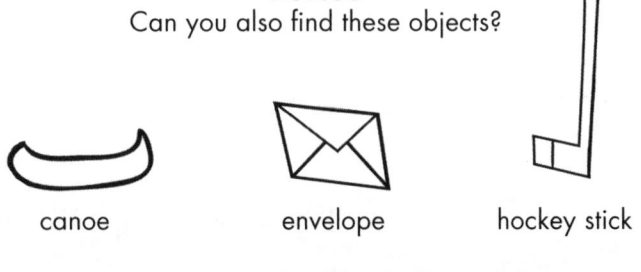

canoe

envelope

hockey stick

# City Subway

Art by Bill Golliher

Flip the page!

# City Subway

*Write the object names in the numbered spaces. For example, if you found the fish first, write "fish" in the first blank.*

The most interesting things happen when I

ride the subway to work! Because I work at

_____ & Associates all the way across
          1

town on _____ Avenue, I get to talk
              2

to lots of different passengers. Just yesterday a

_____ was sitting across from me
          3

holding a unique-looking _____. I
                                    4

asked her, "Where did you get that?" And she said,

"At the _____ shop next to that old
              5

_____ on Tyler Street." Who would
          6

have thought? My favorite part about riding the

subway is when the _____-playing

7

monkey and saxophone-playing _____

8

get on. They never forget to play "Singing in

the _____" and "What a Beautiful

9

_____." Those are the best songs

10

they know. Tomorrow I hope to run into a friendly

_____ who can recommend a good

11

_____. Riding the subway sure is

12

an adventure!

29

# Hidden Pictures®

Write a number below each object based on the order in which you find it in the big picture. Then flip the page to create a silly story with the objects!

pointy hat

olive

game piece

flashlight

golf club

nail

frying pan

crescent moon

chili pepper

snowman

worm

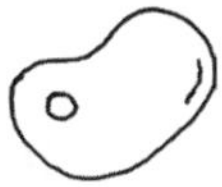

paint palette

## BONUS
Can you also find these objects?

arrowhead

envelope

propeller hat

# First Plane Ride

Art by Scot Ritchie

Flip the page! ↘

# First Plane Ride

*Write the object names in the numbered spaces. For example, if you found the olive first, write "olive" in the first blank.*

Dad told me not to sweat it as we watched each

_____ take off from the runway. I took a
1

deep breath but still felt a big _____ in
2

my stomach. I was about to board my first flight. The

_____ attendant called our boarding
3

group and I handed him my _____. He
4

smiled and gave me a pin with wings that said "Junior

_____." When Dad and I found our seats,
5

Dad said I could sit by the _____. After I
6

had buckled my _____, the plane began
7

to move. I felt like I was on a roller coaster because

of the way my _____ did a summersault.

8

Then we were in the air, and it wasn't scary at all!

The cars below looked like toys from way up here

as we disappeared into a puffy _____.

9

The plane even served my favorite snack, a salted

_____. Later, when we landed on the

10

_____, I was ready to go again. I can't

11

wait for the _____ ride home!

12

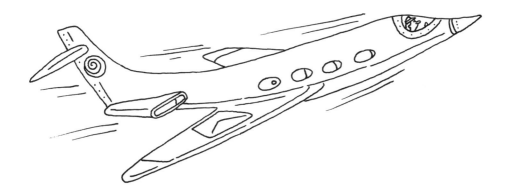

# Hidden Pictures®

Write a number below each object based on the order in which you find it in the big picture. Then flip the page to create a silly story with the objects!

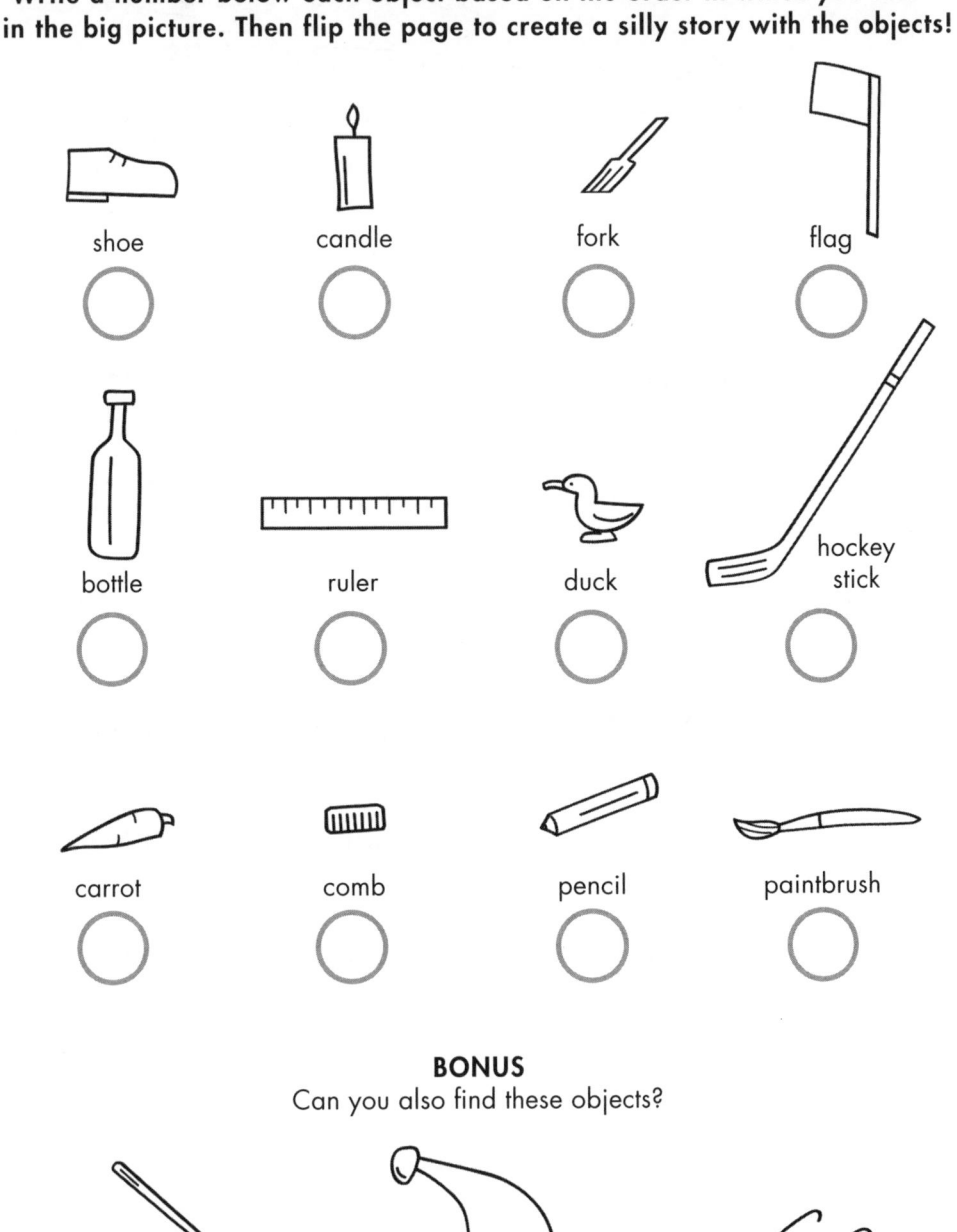

shoe ◯

candle ◯

fork ◯

flag ◯

bottle ◯

ruler ◯

duck ◯

hockey stick ◯

carrot ◯

comb ◯

pencil ◯

paintbrush ◯

**BONUS**
Can you also find these objects?

needle

elf's hat

eyeglasses

# Doggy Paddling

Flip the page!

# Doggy Paddling

*Write the object names in the numbered spaces. For example, if you found the comb first, write "comb" in the first blank.*

Lake _____ is exactly 150 pawsteps from
1

our dog cabin. Down at the _____, Pa
2

and I jump into our prized _____, grab
3

our yellow paddles, and start off across the glistening

_____. As I start paddling with my
4

_____, a loud _____ noise
5        6

erupts behind me. I look back, and my dad is howling

with laughter because I accidentally splashed him with

the _____! He reaches in the water and
7

splashes me back. Now we both look like a soggy

_____. Pa suddenly whispers, "Look,

<u>8</u>

there's a rare striped _____!" I look

<u>9</u>

over to see a flash of _____ fins swish

<u>10</u>

underwater. We do a _____ dive into

<u>11</u>

the lake in hopes of catching it, but just as quickly as

it showed up, it swims behind the _____.

<u>12</u>

Pa says, "Well, maybe next time we should wear our

bathing suits!"

# Hidden Pictures®

Write a number below each object based on the order in which you find it in the big picture. Then flip the page to create a silly story with the objects!

glove

cotton swab

toy top

dog bone

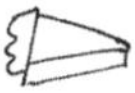

○  ○  ○  ○

pie

teacup

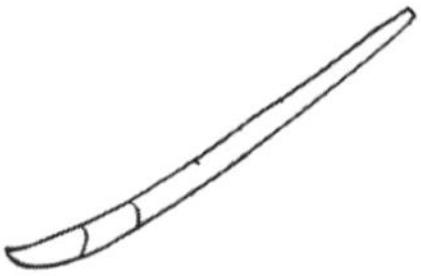

paintbrush

muffin

○  ○  ○  ○

sailboat

feather duster

candle

mushroom

○  ○  ○  ○

**BONUS**
Can you also find this object?

carrot

# Camping Catastrophe

**Flip the page!**

# Camping Catastrophe

*Write the object names in the numbered spaces. For example, if you found the muffin first, write "muffin" in the first blank.*

When we pulled up to the _____ site, I
<sub>1</sub>

immediately jumped out of the _____.
<sub>2</sub>

We had finally made it! My family and I were here

from _____ City to enjoy the great
<sub>3</sub>

outdoors. I pulled out the _____ spray
<sub>4</sub>

and flashlights as we unpacked while dad grabbed

the tent. "_____!" he shouted. Panic
<sub>5</sub>

washed over his _____. "What's wrong?"
<sub>6</sub>

I asked. "I think I forgot the tent poles," he said. My

sisters and I looked at him in disbelief. We all dug

through the camp pile like raccoons digging through

a _____ bin, but the tent poles were
    7

nowhere to be found. Dad decided he'd drive to the

closest _____ store to find something to
            8

hold up our tent while the rest of us set up a blazing

_____ to roast marshmallows for
        9

s'mores. Suddenly, I felt a huge _____
                                                    10

fall from the darkening sky.

We must have looked so

silly huddling under a giant

_____ to stay dry.
        11

Next time we'd better camp

out in our _____!
                12

# Hidden Pictures®

Write a number below each object based on the order in which you find it in the big picture. Then flip the page to create a silly story with the objects!

hamburger
◯

sock
◯

tomato
◯

trowel
◯

watermelon
◯

crayon
◯

umbrella
◯

game piece
◯

key
◯

boomerang
◯

cinnamon bun
◯

drumstick
◯

**BONUS**
Can you also find this object?

wedge of lemon

# Sea Pig

Flip the page!

# Sea Pig

*Write the object names in the numbered spaces. For example, if you found the drumstick first, write "drumstick" in the first blank.*

Today marks my fifteenth anniversary as a deep

_____ explorer. My friends thought

      1

I was nuts when I accepted the job. They said,

"_____ pigs don't belong in the

      2

water!" But there really is no other place I'd rather

be than in my yellow _____. You see,

           3

whenever I take a deep-sea dive into the great

blue _____, it's like I become one

    4

with the swimming _____ fish and

        5

beautiful _____ urchins. I'll never

    6

forget the time I was trying to locate the world's

largest sea _____. It has a big thorny
                    7

_____ with the meanest looking
        8

_____ along its tail. Needless to say,
        9

what I ended up discovering was just as exciting. A

sunken _____ full of gold was laying at
                10

the bottom of the ocean! I nearly jumped out of my

_____. As for the thorny sea creature,
        11

that remains an unsolved _____.
                                12

# Hidden Pictures®

Write a number below each object based on the order in which you find it in the big picture. Then flip the page to create a silly story with the objects!

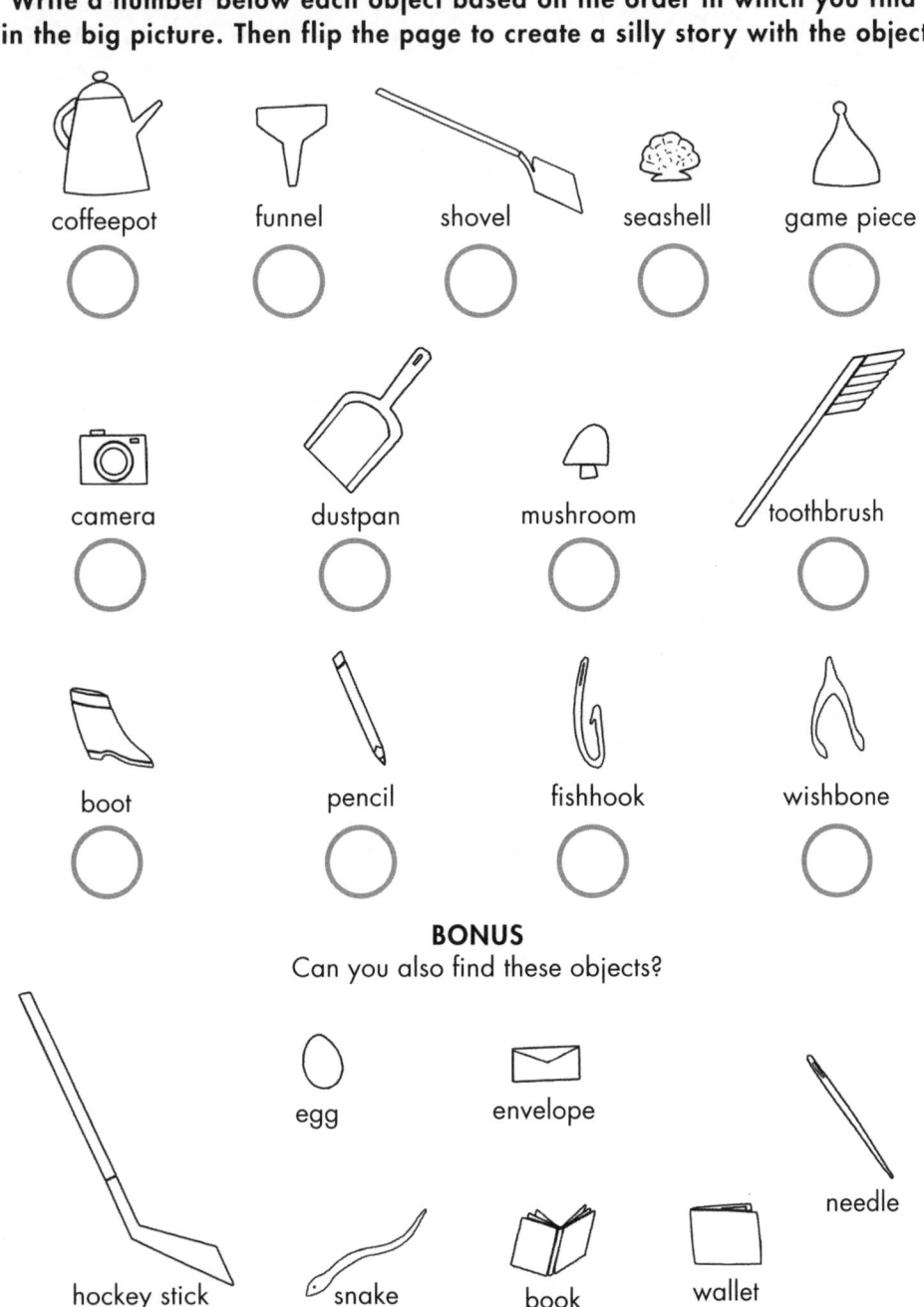

coffeepot ◯

funnel ◯

shovel ◯

seashell ◯

game piece ◯

camera ◯

dustpan ◯

mushroom ◯

toothbrush ◯

boot ◯

pencil ◯

fishhook ◯

wishbone ◯

## BONUS
Can you also find these objects?

egg

envelope

needle

hockey stick

snake

book

wallet

# Just in Time

Art by Gary Mohrman

Flip the page!

# Just in Time

*Write the object names in the numbered spaces. For example, if you found the seashell first, write "seashell" in the first blank.*

"All aboard the Central _____!" Just as I
<u>1</u>

made it to the platform the conductor was making the

final call to Fort _____. What a morning
<u>2</u>

I had trying to get to the _____ station
<u>3</u>

on time. My alarm _____ was set for
<u>4</u>

p.m. instead of a.m. When I woke up an hour late, I

jumped out of my _____ faster than a
<u>5</u>

bolt of lightning. I had just enough time to brush my

_____, comb my _____,
<u>6</u>                          <u>7</u>

and put on my tie. I was rushing so fast I forgot I

was still wearing my _____! I left my

house and ran to the _____ to hail a

_____ to the station. When the driver

pulled up I said, "Step on the _____.

I've got a _____ to catch!" A dozen

red lights later, we finally made it. As I ran out of

the car, the driver shouted, "Sir, you forgot your

_____!" It's a good thing he did,

otherwise I wouldn't have gotten very far without it!

# Hidden Pictures®

Write a number below each object based on the order in which you find it in the big picture. Then flip the page to create a silly story with the objects!

bell

shoe

ring

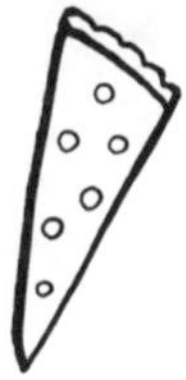

pizza

○    ○    ○    ○

fishhook

baseball bat

ruler

broom

○    ○    ○    ○

bird

golf club

ladder

sailboat

teacup

○    ○    ○    ○    ○

**BONUS**
Can you also find this object?

phone

# Beach Bound

Flip the page!

# Beach Bound

*Write the object names in the numbered spaces. For example, if you found the shoe first, write "shoe" in the first blank.*

" . . . Out came the _____ and dried

1

up all the rain, so the itsy-bitsy _____

2

climbed up the _____ again!" That's the

3

fiftieth time we've sung "Itsy-Bitsy _____,"

4

my baby sister's favorite song. This is Abby's first

time going to _____ Beach, and I have

5

lots to show her when we get there. First, we'll look

for seashells down by the _____ and

6

pretend we're on a _____ hunt! Then,

7

when our buckets are full, we'll grab our inflatable

_____ and go for a swim with Dad. I'll
    8

show Abby how to test the water out by sticking one

_____ in at a time. After that we'll head
    9

back to our _____ chairs and build a
                    10

really big _____. Last time mine was
                11

taller than a _____! Well, five more
                    12

miles to go. I can't wait to feel the _____
                                            13

between my toes!

# Hidden Pictures®

Write a number below each object based on the order in which you find it in the big picture. Then flip the page to create a silly story with the objects!

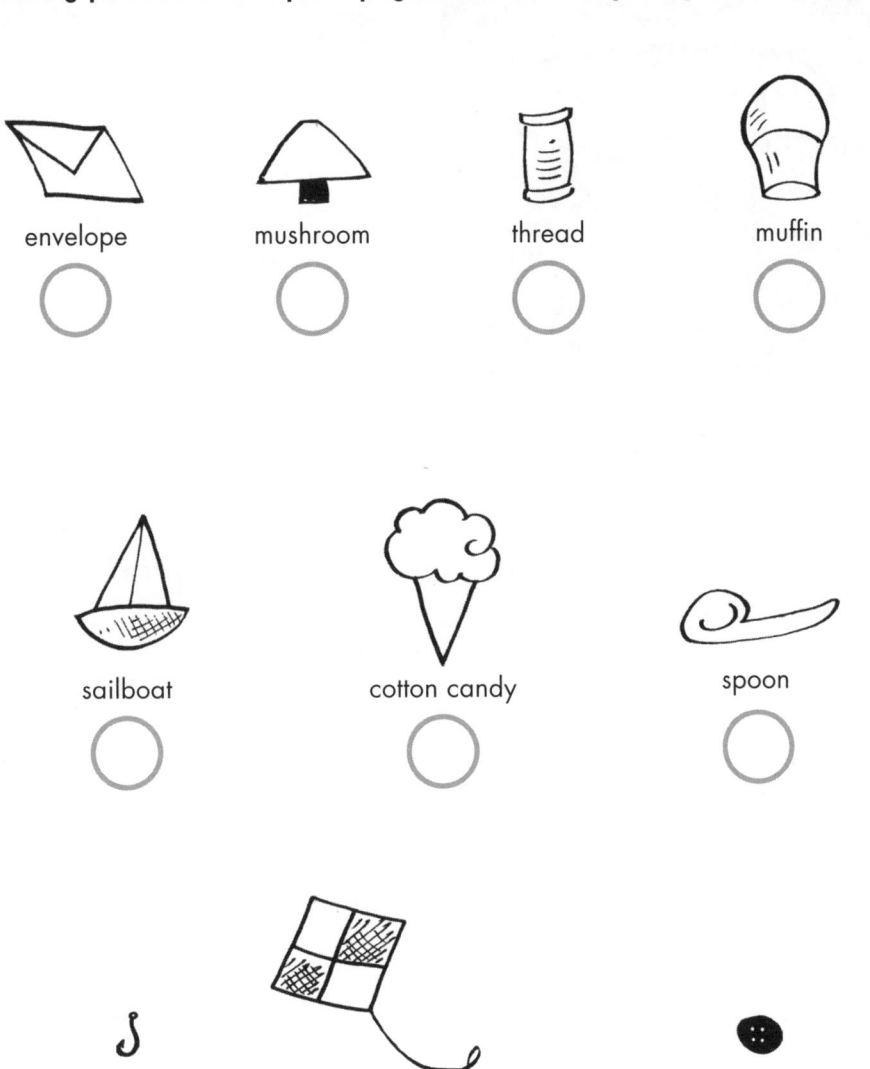

envelope

mushroom

thread

muffin

sailboat

cotton candy

spoon

fishhook

kite

button

# Up, Up, and Away

Flip the page!

# Up, Up, and Away

*Write the object names in the numbered spaces. For example, if you found the cotton candy first, write "cotton candy" in the first blank.*

"The _____ is the limit." That's what I
1

always say. I decided to turn that into a reality at the

annual _____ Balloon Festival when
2

my friend and I took a hot-air _____
3

ride over _____ Park. As we stepped
4

into the wicker basket, the attendant handed us a

large _____ filled with birdseed. She
5

said, "If you hold your arm out steady when you're

in the sky, the _____ birds will fly over
6

to you and eat right out of your paw!" She then

gave the _____ signal to our balloon
7

pilot and we were off the ground. As we lifted

higher and higher in the sky, we started hearing

a strange _____ noise. It was as if a
8

giant _____ was heading right toward
9

us. Suddenly we were surrounded by a huge flock

of birds! I scooped up some birdseed, held out my

_____, and the birds went wild. When
10

the balloon finally landed, I couldn't wait to put my

paws back on the ground!

# Hidden Pictures®

Write a number below each object based on the order in which you find it in the big picture. Then flip the page to create a silly story with the objects!

screwdriver
◯

teacup
◯

pennant
◯

boot
◯

squeegee
◯

banana
◯

candle
◯

flashlight
◯

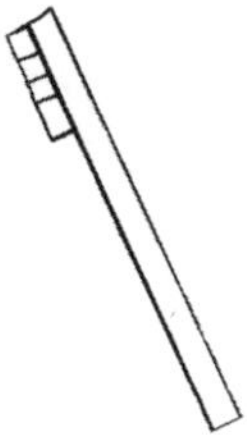

toothbrush
◯

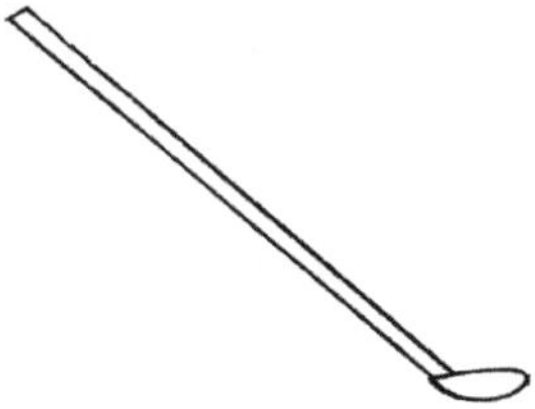

golf club
◯

sock
◯

**BONUS**
Can you also find these objects?

umbrella

tack

# The Missing Keys

Art by Chuck Dillon

Flip the page!

# The Missing Keys

*Write the object names in the numbered spaces. For example, if you found the screwdriver first, write "screwdriver" in the first blank.*

"Stop what you're doing!" said my mom. "We have

a serious _____. I can't find the car
                    **1**

keys." We were in the middle of packing up the

_____ for our trip to _____
            **2**                              **3**

Harbor when Mom realized she packed the keys

somewhere. "We need to search every backpack,

_____, and suitcase!" We emptied out
            **4**

the trunk and frantically searched our belongings.

Dad dumped out everything—clothes, underwear,

_____ gear, _____ chargers,
            **5**                          **6**

soap—they were all scattered across our driveway.

Rufus even sniffed around the _____.
                                          7

(Alex got bored of looking and started snacking on

a _____.) "Hey, guys?" Mom said with
              8

a nervous laugh. "Wouldn't you know . . . the keys

were in my _____ pocket the whole time."
                        9

Dad let out a big laugh and said, "Well, nothing like a

_____ drill first thing in the morning! Ok,
          10

first one to finish re-packing their bags can pick the

_____ we're listening to!"
          11

# Answers

## On the cover!

## Page 1

There are 5 bananas, 4 carrots, and 3 pizzas in this pad.

There are the most canoes hidden (4).

The mitten is on page 15, the glove is on page 39, the sock is on page 43, and the propeller hat is on page 31.

## 3 Road Trip

## 7 Setting Sail

## 11 Space Explorers

## 15 Happy Trails

# Answers

**19** To Grandma's House

**23** Great Bear Lodge

**27** City Subway

**31** First Plane Ride

**35** Doggy Paddling

**39** Camping Catastrophe

# Answers

**43** Sea Pig

**47** Just In Time

**51** Beach Bound

**55** Up, Up, and Away

**59** The Missing Keys

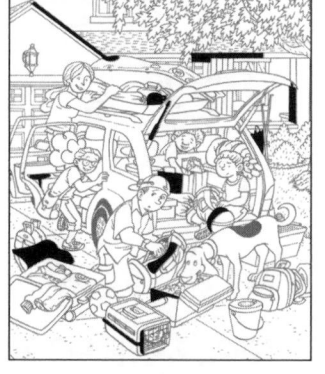